HALLOWEEN SHORT STORIES FOR KIDS

DISCOVER SPOOKY TALES AND ADVENTURES FOR KIDS

AGES 6-10

Evelyn Shadowborne.

Copyright © 2023 by Evelyn Shadowborne

All rights reserved.

No part of this publication may be reproduced, distributed, or transmitted in any form or by any means, including photocopying, recording, or other electronic or mechanical methods, without the prior written permission of the publisher, except in the case of brief quotations embodied in critical reviews and certain other non-commercial uses permitted by copyright law.

Legal Notice:

The stories, characters, and events depicted in this book, "Halloween short stories for kids " are entirely fictional. Any resemblance to actual persons, living or dead, or events is purely coincidental.

Disclaimer:

The author and publisher have made every effort to ensure the accuracy of the information presented in this book. However, they assume no responsibility for errors, omissions, or suitability for any particular purpose. The stories in this book are intended for entertainment purposes only and should not be used as a substitute for professional advice or guidance.

ACKNOWLEDGMENT

The stories contained in this book are the original work of Evelyn Shadowborne, created to entertain and inspire young readers. The characters, settings, and plots are products of the author's imagination and creative license.

Reader Discretion

Parents and guardians are advised to review the content of this book before sharing it with children. Some stories may contain mildly spooky or suspenseful elements that might not be suitable for very young readers or those easily frightened.

ACKNOWLEDGMENT	3
THE ENCHANTED PUMPKIN PATCH	6
THE MISCHIEVOUS GHOST AT SCHOOL	16
THE ENCHANTED HALLOWEEN COSTUME	24
THE WITCH'S MYSTERIOUS BREW	31
THE FRIENDLY MONSTER UNDER THE BED	38
THE ADVENTURES IN THE SPOOKY FOREST	44
THE CURSED CANDY HOUSE	51
THE HAUNTED CARNIVAL	57
THE GHOSTLY TREASURE HUNT	64
THE SPECTRAL MASQUERADE BALL	70
SECRET OF THE CREEPY MANSION	76
THE NIGHT OF THE LIVING TOYS	83
THE HAUNTED HAYRIDE ADVENTURE	89
THE GHOST SHIP IN MOONLIGHT BAY	95

THE ENCHANTED
PUMPKIN PATCH

At the outskirts of the charming town of Spookville, nestled among ancient oak trees, lay the Enchanted Pumpkin Patch. Each year, as Halloween approached, the pumpkins in this patch would come alive. Their eyes glowed like glowing embers, and playful smiles adorned their faces.

One sunny autumn afternoon, a group of curious children from Spookville Elementary School decided to explore the mysterious legend of the Enchanted Pumpkin Patch. Among them were siblings, Alex and Lily, along with their friends, Emily, Charlie, and Mike. They had heard tales about the pumpkins whispering riddles and playing tricks on anyone who dared to venture into the patch after dark.

As the children arrived at the entrance of the patch, they were greeted by a creaky old sign that read,

"Enter if you dare!"

The group's bravest member, Alex, took a big breath and stepped in first, with the rest following quickly behind. They were armed with flashlights, determined to uncover the truth behind the spooky rumors.

The once cheerful orange pumpkins now looked eerie as they came to life. The children's excitement was mixed with a hint of trepidation as they approached the first pumpkin. "Greetings," Lily said tentatively. To their amazement, the pumpkin winked at her and said, "Welcome, young ones, to the Enchanted Pumpkin Patch.

Solve my riddle, and a sweet treat you shall find!"

The children exchanged glances, excitement bubbling within them. "Alright, we're up for the challenge!" declared Emily confidently.

The pumpkin grinned and posed its riddle, "I have a radiant smile, but I'm not the sun. I appear in October when the spooky fun's begun. What am I?"

After a few moments of thoughtful silence, Charlie exclaimed, "It's a jack-o'-lantern!"

The pumpkin clapped its leafy hands, and suddenly, a hidden compartment beneath it opened, revealing a basket of delectable candies. The children cheered and shared the treats, feeling more at ease now that they had passed the first test.

As they ventured deeper into the patch, they encountered more animated pumpkins, each with its own riddle to challenge them. The pumpkins seemed to relish the company of the curious children, revealing stories of Halloween traditions and ancient legends.

One pumpkin, named Oliver, told them about the magical pumpkin that granted wishes to those who found it. Another pumpkin, Henrietta, shared a tale of friendship between a kind scarecrow and a lonely pumpkin. The children were mesmerized by these enchanting stories and made a mental note to remember them for their upcoming Halloween celebrations.

Hours passed, and the sun began to set, casting long shadows across the pumpkin patch. But the children determined to continue their adventure, even in the dark. Guided by the glowing pumpkins, they reached the heart of the patch, where the legendary Great Pumpkin resided.

The Great Pumpkin was colossal, with eyes that sparkled like distant stars. "Congratulations, brave souls, for making it this far," boomed the Great Pumpkin's voice, deep and resonant.

The children exchanged glances, excitement and nervousness filling the air. "Thank you," Alex replied, trying to keep his voice steady.

"We're here to learn about the Enchanted Pumpkin Patch's secrets"

The Great Pumpkin nodded approvingly. "Then prove your worth with one final challenge. Solve my riddle, and you shall earn the title of Pumpkin Pioneers!"

The children took a deep breath, ready to face whatever came their way. The Great Pumpkin's riddle echoed through the patch, "In the darkest hour, I come out to play. I fly through the night, and at dawn, I fade away. What am I?"

They pondered for a moment until Lily's eyes lit up. "It's a bat!"

The Great Pumpkin chuckled, impressed by their knowledge. "Correct! You have shown courage and wisdom on this All Hallows' Eve. As a reward, I grant you the knowledge of the Pumpkin Patch's magic."

The Great Pumpkin leaned forward, and a soft glow enveloped the children. It was a magical sensation, as if they were being embraced by the very essence of Halloween itself. The Great

Pumpkin revealed the secrets of the patch - how it came to life every Halloween to spread joy and mischief, and how it held the power to inspire imagination in those who dared to explore its mysteries.

With newfound knowledge and a sense of wonder, the children thanked the Great Pumpkin and bid farewell to their newfound pumpkin friends. As they left the Enchanted Pumpkin Patch, they felt a mix of excitement and gratitude for the unforgettable adventure they had experienced.

From that day on, the children of Spookville cherished the memories of their encounter with the living pumpkins. They shared the tales they had learned with their families and friends, igniting a newfound fascination with Halloween's magic throughout the town.

As Halloween night arrived, the children put on their costumes and gathered at the edge of the Enchanted Pumpkin Patch. With a twinkle in their eyes, they recalled the riddles and stories, passing down the traditions to younger generations. Together, they celebrated the enchanting spirit of Halloween, knowing that magic resided not just in the pumpkins but in their hearts as well.

And so, the legend of the Enchanted Pumpkin Patch lived on, bringing joy and excitement to the young tricksters of Spookville year after year. The children understood that Halloween was not just about scary creatures and candy but about the sense of wonder and camaraderie that came with sharing magical moments together.

As they gazed at the stars above, the children felt a profound connection to the spirit of Halloween. They knew that the enchantment of this night would remain with them forever, guiding them through life's adventures and filling their hearts with the magic of imagination.

And so, dear readers, as you celebrate Halloween this year, remember the tale of the Enchanted Pumpkin Patch and the young adventurers who discovered its secrets. Embrace the magic of this special night, and may the spirit of Halloween fill your hearts with joy.

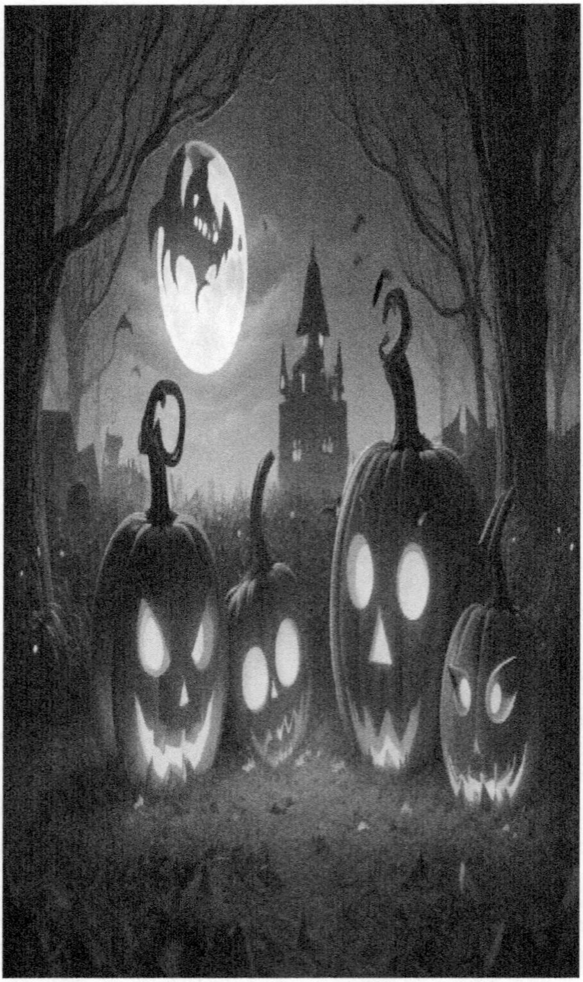

THE MISCHIEVOUS GHOST

AT SCHOOL

In the town of Spookville, the children had their share of thrills in the Haunted Pumpkin Patch. However, the excitement did not stop there, for Halloween had more surprises in store. Soon, they discovered a mischievous ghost wandering the halls of Spookville Elementary School.

It all commenced on a crisp October morning, just a few days before Halloween. As the children settled into their classrooms, peculiar incidents caught their attention. Books floated off shelves, chairs moved on their own, and eerie laughter echoed through the corridors. The school seemed to come alive with supernatural activity.

One day, Emily arrived early at school to assist her teacher with preparations for the Halloween party. As she entered the classroom, she spotted a faint, glowing figure hovering near the chalkboard. "Hello?" she called out cautiously.

The ghost turned to face her, its transparent form wavering in the air. "Greetings, young one. I am Casper, the mischievous school ghost," it said, with a sly grin.

Emily was astonished but remained brave. "What do you want?" she asked, trying to sound confident.

Casper chuckled, "Oh, just a bit of fun, my dear. You see, I've been haunting this school for centuries, and Halloween is my favorite time to play tricks on everyone."

Emily's curiosity got the better of her, and she asked, "What kind of tricks?"

Casper floated closer to her and whispered, "I hide things, rearrange furniture, and create spooky illusions. But fear not, my intentions are to bring smiles to your faces."

True to his word, Casper's pranks were more amusing than scary. He made the school's mascot dance in the hallways, turned the water in the drinking fountains into orange-colored "potion," and caused the cafeteria tables to do a little jig during lunchtime.

Word of the friendly ghost quickly spread, and soon, Alex, Lily, Charlie, and Mike also encountered Casper during their school days. The ghost even helped them with their Halloween decorations, creating breathtakingly spooky displays that amazed the entire school.

However, not everyone was delighted with Casper's antics. Mr. Thompson, the stern school principal, firmly believed that the children were responsible for all the commotion. He decided to set up traps to catch the "culprits" and put an end to the supposed mischief.

The children realized they needed to help Casper and prove his innocence. They devised a plan to lead Mr. Thompson to the truth without revealing the ghost's presence. They set up a concealed camera to capture Casper in action while ensuring he stayed safely hidden from view.

On the night of the Halloween party, the children executed their plan. As Mr.

Thompson monitored the school through the security cameras, he was astonished to witness chairs moving, decorations coming to life, and strange apparitions appearing in the hallways. He couldn't believe his eyes and was left with no explanation for the supernatural occurrences.

Finally, the camera captured Casper floating past the lens, his ethereal glow unmistakable. The children had succeeded in proving Casper's existence without compromising his secret.

Armed with the evidence, they confronted Mr. Thompson the next day. To everyone's surprise, he wasn't angry; instead, he was in awe of the magical discovery. He apologized for suspecting the children and embraced the spirit of Halloween. From then on, he became an ally, helping to keep Casper's secret and ensuring the school embraced the festive spirit.

As Halloween night approached, the school hosted a grand party where Casper's pranks became the highlight of the event. The students, teachers, and even Mr. Thompson joined in the fun, laughing and dancing with the friendly ghost.

And so, Casper the mischievous school ghost became an integral part of Spookville Elementary School's Halloween tradition. He brought joy and laughter to everyone and continued to be a beloved, albeit invisible, member of the school community.

The legend of Casper, the friendly school ghost, lives on in the hearts of the children of Spookville. They fondly remember the year they encountered a ghostly friend who taught them the true meaning of Halloween - to embrace the magic of the unknown and

the joy of sharing laughter with friends,
both seen and unseen.

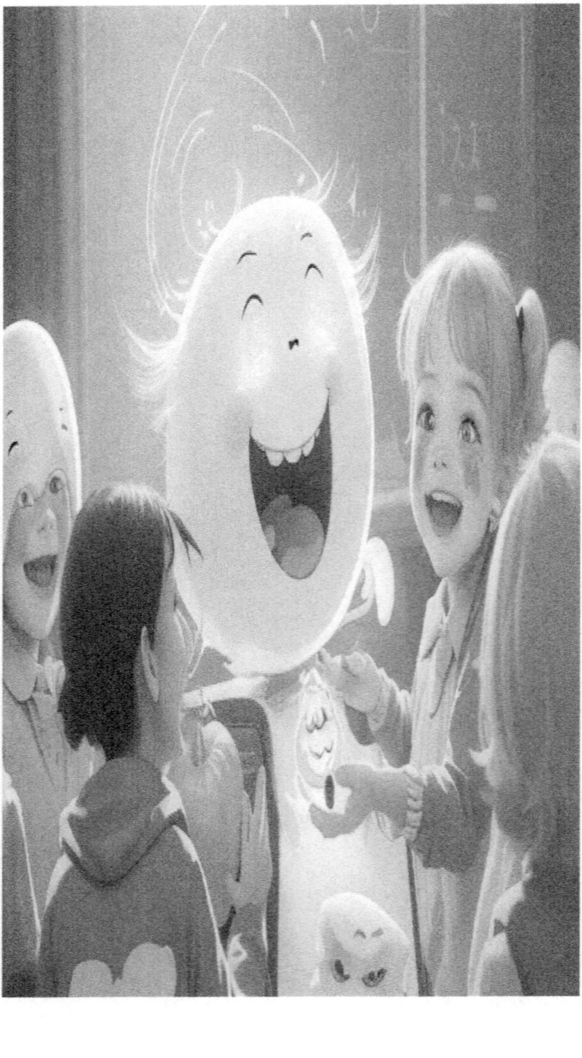

THE ENCHANTED HALLOWEEN COSTUME

As Halloween approached, the young residents of Spookville couldn't contain their anticipation. The streets adorned with eerie decorations, and the air filled with the scent of pumpkin spice and candy treats. Amidst the festive ambiance, the children eagerly awaited the moment to choose their Halloween costumes.

One sunny afternoon, they congregated at Lily's house, where her grandmother, Mrs. Goodwin, was renowned for crafting the most magical and captivating costumes in town. Mrs. Goodwin's creations were said to possess a touch of genuine enchantment, transforming the wearers into the very characters they portrayed.

The children perused a treasure trove of costumes in Mrs. Goodwin's attic. Among them were capes that bestowed invisibility, hats that granted flight, and gloves that conjured mesmerizing illusions. Each costume held its distinct allure, but one, in particular, captivated their attention - the "Attire of Whimsical Wonders."

The Attire of Whimsical Wonders was an ornate ensemble adorned with twinkling stars and mystical symbols. Mrs. Goodwin explained that when someone wore this costume, they would temporarily possess the ability to manifest their wildest dreams into reality.

The children were incredulous. "You mean, if I wear this costume, my imaginations can come true?" asked Emily, her eyes gleaming with excitement.

"Yes, my dear," replied Mrs. Goodwin with a warm smile. "But remember, magic must be wielded responsibly. The Attire of Whimsical Wonders is a gift, and it is crucial to exercise wisdom in its use."

Alex, Lily, Emily, Charlie, and Mike deliberated on who should don the magical attire. After much discussion, they decided that Emily, with her vivid imagination and kind heart, would be the perfect candidate.

As Emily donned the Attire of Whimsical Wonders, a tingling sensation coursed through her body. She felt an exhilarating surge of power, as if she could reach out and touch the stars themselves. Excitement and responsibility intermingled within her, as she now held the key to a realm of boundless possibilities.

The children gathered in the backyard, and Emily focused on her first wish.

She exclaimed "I want a magical tea party with talking animals."

To their astonishment, the yard transformed before their eyes. A table adorned with delectable treats appeared, and animals of various shapes and sizes converged. Squirrels engaged in conversations with birds, rabbits shared tea with hedgehogs, and even a wise owl joined the enchanting gathering.

Laughter and joy filled the air as the children engaged in delightful conversations with their newfound animal friends. They knew that this magical moment would be etched in their memories forever.

As the day turned to evening, the children continued to explore the wonders of the enchanted attire. They embarked on journeys to distant lands, encountered legendary creatures, and even traversed imaginary worlds inspired by their favorite storybooks. Each adventure surpassed the last in excitement, and Emily reveled in the joy of bringing her friends' dreams to life.

However, as the night wore on, Emily began to comprehend the importance of balance and responsibility. The magic was incredibly potent, and it was vital not to let it overpower her judgment.

As the clock struck midnight, the Attire of Whimsical Wonders began to shimmer, signaling the end of its enchantment. Emily thanked her friends for the incredible experiences and reluctantly removed the attire.

She shared her newfound wisdom with her friends, emphasizing that magic was a precious gift to be utilized for spreading happiness, rather than indulging in every fleeting whim.

In the days that followed, the children reflected on their adventures with fondness, cherishing the profound lessons they had imbibed. They realized that true magic existed not only in costumes or spells but in the bonds of friendship, the boundless realm of imagination, and the joy of turning dreams into reality.

As Halloween night approached, the children of Spookville donned their chosen costumes and set out for a night of trick-or-treating and merriment. And although they didn't possess the Attire of Whimsical Wonders, they carried the enchantment of that extraordinary day in their hearts, knowing that the spirit of Halloween was more magical than any costume could ever express.

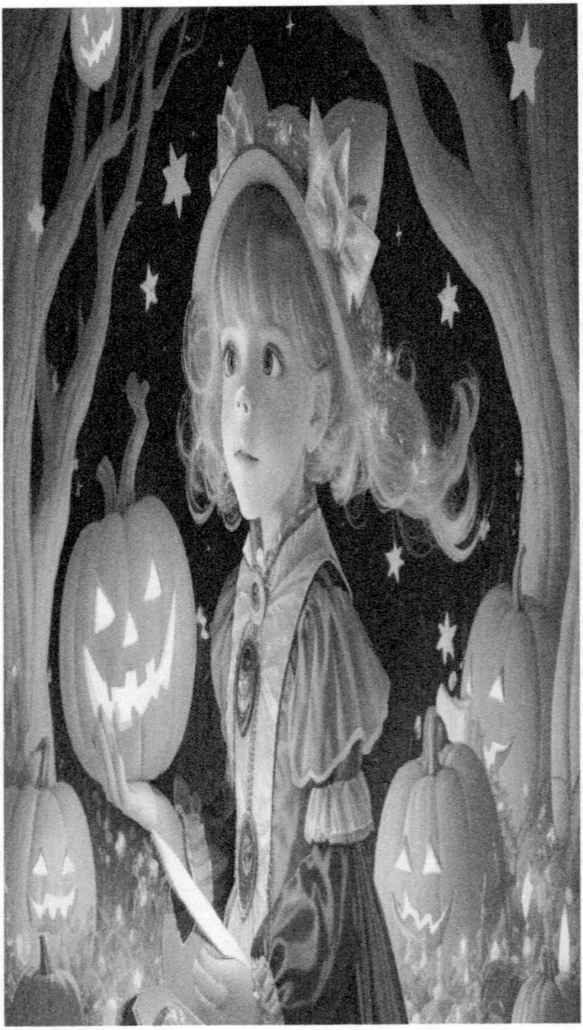

THE WITCH'S MYSTERIOUS BREW

Halloween night arrived in Spookville, shrouding the town in an eerie mist. The children, dressed in their creative costumes, roamed the dimly lit streets with excitement in their hearts. They laughed and collected candies, savoring the spooky ambiance of the night.

As the clock struck nine, the children found themselves in front of an old, mysterious house at the edge of town. The house belonged to the reclusive witch, Madame Esmeralda, who was known for her potent potions and enigmatic demeanor.

Curiosity got the better of the children, and they decided to approach the house. The flickering candles in the windows and the strange shadows dancing on the walls filled them with both fear and fascination.

Taking a deep breath, Alex stepped forward and knocked on the door. Creaking sounds echoed through the house, and moments later, the door swung open to reveal Madame Esmeralda herself. She was draped in a flowing black robe, and her silver hair cascaded down her shoulders like a mystical waterfall.

"What brings you here on this enchanted night?" she asked, her voice as soft as a whisper.

"We were wondering if you could tell us a spooky Halloween story or maybe even share a potion recipe," Lily said, trying to sound brave.

Madame Esmeralda chuckled, her eyes twinkling with mischief. "Ah, you seek a tale of magic and mystery, do you? Come inside, and I shall share with you the legend of the Witch's Mysterious Brew."

The children eagerly entered the witch's home, and she led them to a cozy corner by the fireplace. The room was filled with ancient books, potion vials, and curious artifacts that piqued the children's interest.

Madame Esmeralda began her tale, "Long ago, in a time when magic was as abundant as the stars, there lived a young and talented witch named Isabella. She had a deep love for potions and had spent years perfecting her craft."

"One fateful Halloween night," the witch continued, "Isabella decided to create her most ambitious potion yet - the Mysterious Brew. Legends spoke of its ability to grant a single wish to the one who drank it, but it came with a warning. The wish could not be selfish, for such desires could lead to unforeseen consequences."

The children listened intently, their imaginations running wild with the possibilities of such a potion.

Madame Esmeralda continued, "Isabella prepared the ingredients with care and chanted ancient incantations as she stirred the cauldron under the light of the full moon. When the potion was ready, she gazed into its shimmering depths, wondering what her wish should be."

"Isabella thought of riches, fame, and power, but her heart knew that such desires were not true to her nature. Instead, she wished for something that would benefit her entire village - an eternal bountiful harvest to end their struggles with hunger."

The children were captivated by the tale of selflessness and magic. They felt a connection to Isabella's compassionate nature.

"As Isabella's wish was pure and unselfish, the Mysterious Brew granted it with a burst of radiant light. From that day forward, her village thrived with an abundance of crops, and prosperity graced every household."

"But the legend didn't end there," Madame Esmeralda continued. "Isabella's selfless act had sparked something powerful within the Mysterious Brew. It became a beacon for all those who sought to bring goodness to the world."

As the witch concluded the story, she gazed at the children with knowing eyes. "Remember, my young friends, that true magic lies not in the potions we brew or the spells we cast, but in the kindness and selflessness we show to others. The Mysterious Brew teaches us that the most potent magic of all is the magic of the heart."

The children were touched by the lesson and thanked Madame Esmeralda for sharing the tale. They bid her farewell, carrying the essence of the story with them as they continued their Halloween adventure.

As they roamed the streets once more, they couldn't help but feel the enchantment of the night even more deeply. Halloween had transformed from a night of tricks and treats into a celebration of the magic of kindness and selflessness.

The legend of the Witch's Mysterious Brew stayed with the children long after Halloween had passed. They knew that the true essence of magic lay not in the supernatural but in the goodness that resided within each of their hearts.

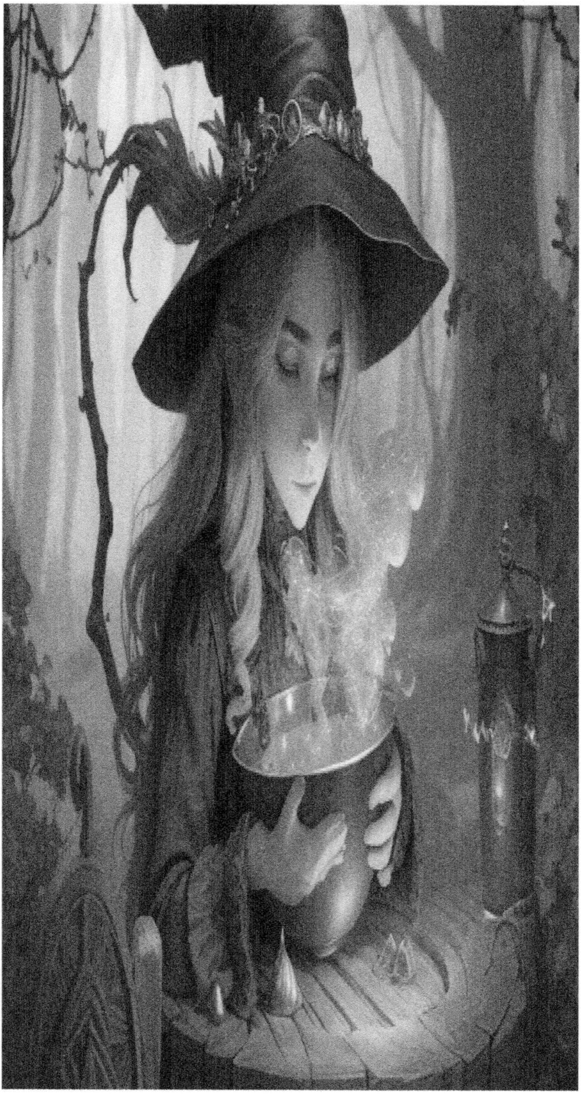

THE FRIENDLY MONSTER
UNDER THE BED

A Rumor of a friendly monster who resided under the bed of a small boy named Timmy grew across Spookville as the kids carried on with their Halloween antics. According to the legends, this monster was different from other others since it was friendly and fun rather than spooky or cunning.

The kids decided to go visit Timmy and his peculiar buddy after hearing about a nice monster. At the end of a dark street, where the eerie glow of Jack-o-lanterns threw odd shadows on the walls, they discovered Timmy's home.

When they knocked on Timmy's door, it opened briefly to reveal a small child with a wide smile.

I'm Timmy, he welcomed cheerfully. Do you want to meet my pal here?

The kids excitedly nodded, their curiosity bubbling, and Timmy led them to his bedroom. They were greeted by a peculiar sight as they entered: a cute little creature with big, round eyes, blue fur, and a fluffy tail. The creature waved at them and smiled.

Timmy introduced his strange acquaintance, "Wuzzy," and stated,

"I'd like you to meet Wuzzy." He is the kindest monster I have ever met.

The kids were wary when they approached Wuzzy, but his kind grin immediately made them feel at ease. Lily shook Wuzzy's hand and said, "Hello, Wuzzy." I'm glad to have met you.

Wuzzy gave her a soft handshake, and the other kids did the same. They found it hard to believe a creature could be so kind and considerate.

Timmy described how he first met Wuzzy.

When I couldn't fall asleep one night, I overheard a quiet moaning under my bed. I was first afraid, but as I turned around, Wuzzy was there. He was equally frightened as I was.

"What did you do then?" Emily questioned.

"I reached out my hand and said, 'its okay, little monster,'" Timmy remarked with a smile. You won't be wounded by me. And from that point forward, we grew close.

Timmy and Wuzzy were inseparable after that. Every night they engaged in games, storytelling, and secret sharing. Wuzzy had grown to be Timmy's devoted protector, making sure that no actual monsters ventured to approach him.

The youngsters were moved by Timmy and Wuzzy's endearing connection. The remainder of the night was spent having fun and joking with the amiable creature under the bed.

The kids said goodbye to Timmy and Wuzzy as Halloween night came to a conclusion, vowing to be back soon. With astonishment and warmth in their hearts, they made their way back to Spookville's center.

As word of the amiable monster spread across the community, additional kids quickly started looking for the enchanted companionship. The once-terrifying notion of monsters under the bed was transformed into a charming story of comradery and faith.

The story of Timmy and Wuzzy persisted over the years. True friends may be discovered in the most unlikely locations, even under their mattresses, according to the youngsters of

Spookville, who grew up cherishing this idea.

Every year on Halloween, Timmy left his door open, inviting kids from all across the community to visit Wuzzy, who remained the most beloved monster in Spookville.

Therefore, when you put yourself to bed on this Halloween night, dear readers, keep in mind the endearing story of Timmy and Wuzzy. They serve as a reminder that genuine friendship knows no boundaries, not even in the realm of magic and monsters.

Don't be alarmed if you ever find yourself awake in bed, listening to ominous noises. Because you never know when a friendly monster could appear and become your most devoted companion.

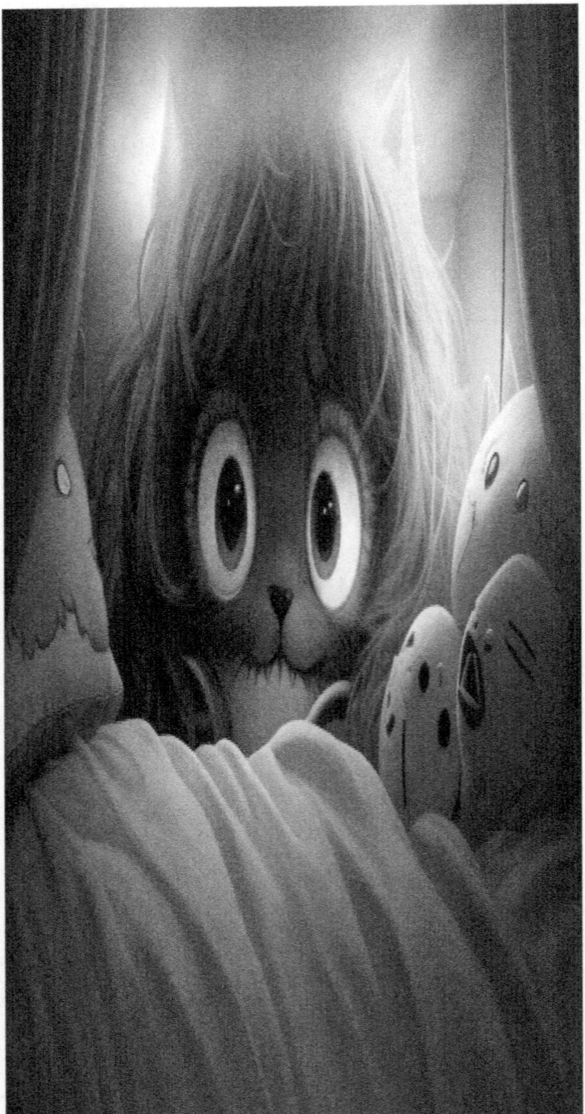

THE ADVENTURES IN THE SPOOKY FOREST

The kids' fascination with a strange forest outside of Spookville grew as the days became shorter and Halloween got closer. The area was referred to as the Spooky Forest because it was supposed to be home to odd animals and unusual noises resonating through the trees.

On the eve of Halloween, Alex, Lily, Emily, Charlie, and Mike gave in to the temptation of the Spooky Forest and went to investigate its mysteries. They entered the dark forest with torches and guts, the crunching of the leaves softening their footfall.

As the kids descended into the forest, it appeared to spring to life. Shadows swirled on the ground, and strange lights flashed amid the trees. The mysticism of the location was enhanced by the wonderful mist that filled the air.

They encountered strange animals that they had only read about in bedtime stories as they ventured farther into the jungle. They were surrounded by a sneaky band of sprites who left dazzling dust in their wake. From the shadows, little gnomes appeared and presented them with wonderful stones and jewels.

One critter in particular drew their interest: Oakley, an amiable talking tree. Oakley had insightful eyes that appeared to contain millennia' worth of knowledge. His voice was loud and resonant, echoing over the jungle as he talked.

Hello, little explorers," said Oakley. What brings you to the Spooky Forest's center on this Halloween eve?

"We've heard tales of the wonders and mysteries of this forest," Lily retorted. We came to have some exhilarating activities as well as see it for ourselves.

You possess the spirit of genuine adventurers, Oakley chuckled. This woodland is full of magic and surprises, but take caution since not everything that glitters is gold.

The youngsters nodded in agreement, their curiosity only mounting. Oakley gave them tips on how to properly travel the jungle and stay away from the sneaky animals' traps.

They came upon a parade of phantoms, ethereal beings dancing in the moonlight, as they continued on their trek. A soft music appeared to emanate from the forest's center as they walked together.

The youngsters arrived at a clearing where a gorgeous unicorn stood after following the heavenly melody. Its horn radiated a gentle brilliance, and its coat glistened like stardust.

With a nod, the unicorn welcomed them and said, "Welcome, young travelers. I am Celestia, the protector of this ethereal world. Your hearts are sincere, and you have good intentions.

What adventure seek you on this wonderful night?

The group's spokesperson was Emily, who said, "We seek the wonders of the Spooky Forest and the joy of experiencing its mysteries."

Then you'll find what you're looking for, Celestia said with a smile. But keep in mind that this forest's magic isn't limited to its magical properties; it also rests in the friendships you make along the road.

Celestia was praised for her advice before the kids carried on with their investigation and a series of amazing experiences. They traveled on the backs of amiable avian creatures, deciphered fairy riddles, and laughed alongside talking animals.

They gathered around a bonfire in the center of the Spooky Forest as the night dragged on. They were joined by the animals they had encountered along the way, creating an astonishing assemblage of magical entities.

Young explorers, we applaud you for embracing the wonder of this night, Oakley added, having accompanied them on their journeys.

Alex said, his eyes beaming with happiness, "And we thank you all for making this Halloween the most unforgettable one yet."

As the kids traveled back to Spookville, the inhabitants of the Spooky Forest bid them farewell. The magic of this night will live with them always since the woodland whispered its secrets in their ears.

The moment they emerged from the Spooky Forest, they were met by the first light of day, signaling the end of Halloween night.

They went home with their hearts full with wonderful memories, anxious to tell their loved ones about their travels. They were aware that the Spooky Forest will always have a particular place in their hearts since it was a location where Halloween spirit and the wonders of imagination coexisted together.

So, my readers, may the escapades of the Spooky Forest serve as an inspiration for you as you celebrate Halloween this year. May you embrace the enchantment that resides in every part of the globe and is just waiting to be found by people with an adventurous spirit.

51

THE CURSED CANDY

HOUSE

The kids of Spookville came across an unsettling sight as Halloween night went on: a mansion made entirely of candy. They were drawn in like moths to a flame by the house's eye-catching hues and enticing fragrance. But something didn't seem right; it was as if an unseen power had forewarned them of the peril that lay within.

The kids approached the Candy House warily, curiosity overriding caution. The home was towering and opulent, with gumdrop windows, licorice doors, and a candy-cane-covered roof. For any youngster with a sweet taste, it appeared like a dream come true, yet there was an obvious atmosphere of evil about it.

The kids came to the front door and saw a sign that said, "Beware! You do so at your own risk. Unfazed, they pushed open the door, which made a foreboding creaking sound. The door slammed shut behind them as soon as they entered, sealing them within the sugar heaven.

This doesn't seem right, Charlie murmured, his voice trembling. We ought to have paid attention to the warning.

The sugar walls started to twist and move before they could respond, creating a maze that seemed to vary with each step they made. Now the sweets seemed like a nefarious trap, drawing them farther into the home.

They spotted a weird person lurking in the shadows as they made their way through the maze. It was a witch with a sinister cackle and melting caramel-colored eyes. She greeted the children, "Welcome, young ones," with a sly grin. You've entered my "cursed Candy House," and there is no getting out.

The kids were terrified, but they knew they had to fight through it and find a way out. If there was a method to lift the curse and get out of the Candy House, they enquired of the witch.

Only those who have love and courage in their hearts can break the spell, the witch cackled once again. You have to successfully complete the sacrifice task, the bravery challenge, and the empathy challenge.

The kids took the witch's challenge with resolve in their eyes. They demonstrated their readiness to give generously by voluntarily giving up part of their sugar pleasures for the challenge of sacrifice.

The test of bravery followed. The kids' nerves were put to the test with unsettling illusions and trickery. They persevered despite their fears by keeping in mind that genuine bravery is the capacity to move forward in the face of dread rather than the absence of fear.

Finally, they faced the difficulty of empathy. The witch envisioned lonely, depressed animals in need of solace. The kids' acts of love and compassion calmed the animals' hearts and lessened their suffering.

The Candy House changed as each task was accomplished. The previously ominous vibe vanished, and the walls changed from being candy to feeling like a warm, welcome house. The witch's evil persona started to disappear, exposing a kind grin.

She answered, "You have broken the spell. "You have shown that you are deserving of leaving the Candy House."

After thanking the witch, the kids went to the front door, which was now wide open. The Candy House collapsed behind them as they exited, leaving nothing but the memory of their incredible meeting.

They understood that the Candy House had not been cursed, but rather those who attempted to take advantage of its sweetness for their own selfish ends. The makeover of the home served as a metaphor for the ability of compassion and generosity to convert the dark into light.

The youngsters experienced a strong feeling of success as they made their way back to Spookville. They had learned important lessons about the value of compassion, bravery, and sacrifice through their time in the Candy House.

They understood that Halloween was about more than just costumes and candy; it was also about embracing the enchantment of unselfish deeds and facing our anxieties.

So, my readers, keep in mind the story of the Cursed Candy House while you celebrate Halloween this year. Embrace the difficulties you face with bravery, understanding, and compassion since it is these traits that have the ability to turn even the most hopeless circumstances into the happiest of times.

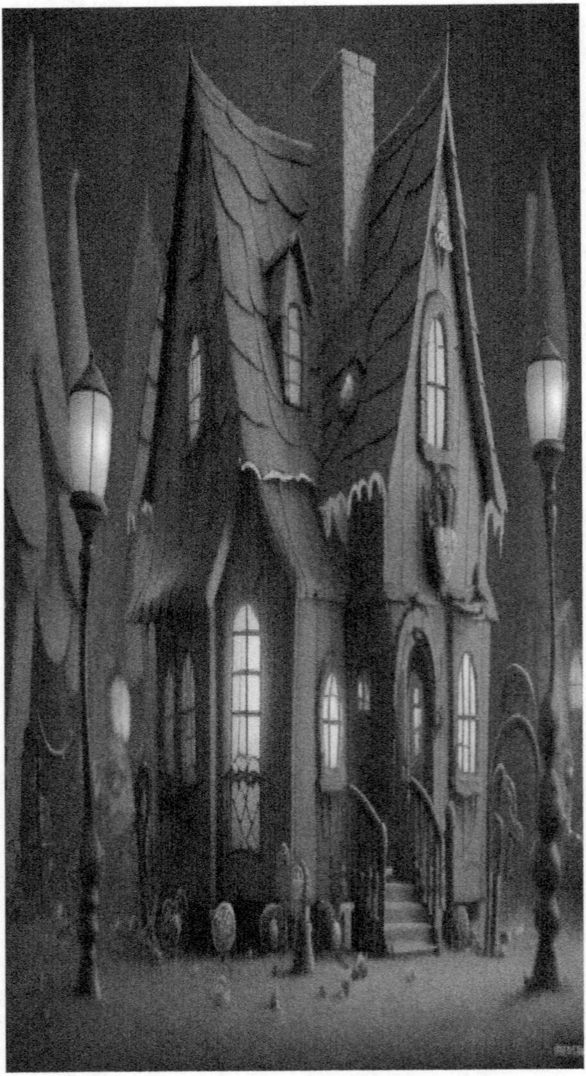

THE HAUNTED CARNIVAL

The youngsters of Spookville heard rumors about a haunting carnival that only arrived once per century as Halloween night went on. The carnival was rumored to have exhilarating rides and enigmatic attractions, but it also held sinister mysteries that tried the bravery of anyone who ventured to enter.

Alex, Lily, Emily, Charlie, and Mike were filled with excitement and dread as they followed the path of ominous lights that led them to the secret location of the haunted carnival.

When they arrived at the carnival grounds, they were met by a plethora of eerie characters, many of whose faces were hidden by the darkness. The aroma of cotton candy blended with a faint undercurrent of something evil, and the air was electrified.

They came into Madame Zara sitting in a shroud of incense and mystery in a fortune teller's tent as they moved deeper into the carnival. She invited the kids to sit before her while her crystal ball shone with an unearthly brightness.

Madame Zara stated in a hauntingly lovely voice, "I see in your eyes a thirst for adventure and a quest for the unknown." Your bravery will be put to the test as the ghostly carnival guides you through the depths of your own anxieties.

The kids looked at each other, understanding that they had gone this far and couldn't go back at this point. They nodded, resolutely determined to meet the trials that lied ahead.

The Haunted House, which is said to be home to haunting apparitions and terrifying thrills, was their first visit. With their flashlights guiding them into the pitch-black, the kids braced themselves and walked through the squeaky doors.

They saw strange sights and noises inside the Haunted House. Ghostly figures appeared to come to life on the walls, and the air was filled with eerie whispering. The kids clung to one other for support as they walked through the eerie maze, refusing to flee out of terror.

They felt a sense of victory as they left the Haunted House. They had confronted their worries and come out of it stronger.

They proceeded to the Carnival Ride of Illusions next on their eerie journey. It was rumored that this rollercoaster played mind games, warped perceptions of reality, and made the impossible appear conceivable.

The youngsters buckled their seatbelts and prepared for the thrill of a lifetime in the spinning carts. The environment shook and rotated around them, almost defying gravity. A multitude of stars encircled them as they found themselves floating in midair before falling back to earth as though they were in free fall.

They lurched out of the rollercoaster with laughing and giddy joy as it eventually came to an end. Their understanding of reality had been tested by The Carnival Ride of Illusions, which also served as a helpful reminder that often the most exceptional experiences may be discovered in the world of imagination.

The House of Mirrors, a labyrinth of mirrored surfaces that played pranks on their reflections, was their last visit. Every mirror showed a distinct reflection of the person looking back, some are exaggerated and amusing and others eerie and spooky.

They confronted their own uncertainties and misgivings as they made their way through the maze. They were forced to face their inner demons since the mirrors appeared to reflect their innermost fears and self-doubts.

They also found strength in the reflections of their bond amid the dizzying mirrors. Together, they understood that nothing was impossible, and that the encouragement of loyal friends was the most effective defense against fear.

The eerie carnival started to vanish as the clock struck midnight, its secrets and enchantments disappearing back into the night. With their hearts overflowing with the memories of a night to never forget, the kids discovered themselves outside the carnival gates.

They were aware that the haunted carnival had served as more than simply a collection of eerie attractions; it had also served as a test of their bravery, a celebration of their friendship, and a gentle reminder that the genuine magic of Halloween rested not in jump scares and frights, but rather in the ties of trust and love.

The kids understood that their experiences at the haunted carnival had helped them mature spiritually and intellectually as they made their way back to Spookville. They had learned that companionship and their innate strength could help them conquer even the most terrifying obstacles.

So, my readers, keep the story of the Haunted Carnival in mind when you celebrate Halloween this year. Accept the unknown, bravely face your anxieties, and treasure the friendships that guide you through the night.

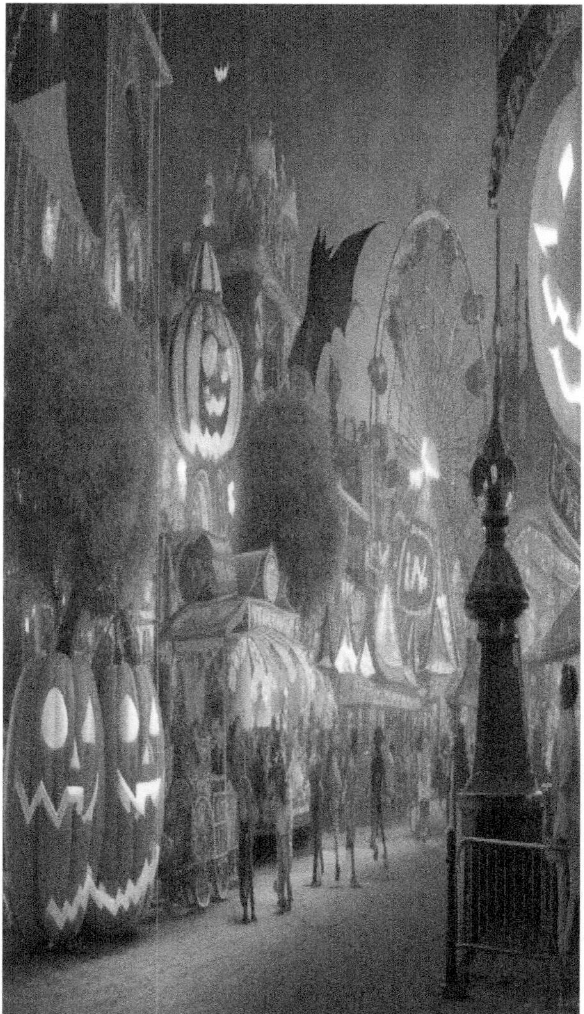

THE GHOSTLY TREASURE HUNT

The youngsters of Spookville discovered a worn treasure map hidden behind a tombstone in the ancient graveyard as Halloween night went on. They felt drawn to the map by its allure of undiscovered riches and eerie experiences.

Alex, Lily, Emily, Charlie, and Mike made the decision to go on a ghostly treasure hunt after being intrigued by the enigmatic map. They navigated through gloomy woodlands, antiquated ruin sites, and neglected cemeteries as they followed the map's enigmatic hints.

The first hint brought them to an eerie cemetery where the gravestones appeared to be whispering something to the breeze. They came upon a ghostly person that was glowing with an ethereal light while they were looking through the graves.

The ghost inquired, its voice resonating with a tinge of melancholy, "Who goes there?"

Alex answered, "We are the children of Spookville, looking for the wealth that is concealed.

"The treasure you seek is not gold or jewels," the ghost said with a nod. The connections of friendship and prior memories are what stand the test of time.

The kids were perplexed but heeded the ghost's advice as they carried on their search.

A forgotten ruin tucked away in the woodland was where they found the second clue. The decaying structures appeared to be whispering legends and tales of long-forgotten civilizations. They discovered a painting that showed a bygone age as they were exploring the ruins.

The youngsters found themselves in the middle of a historical scenario when all of a sudden, the figures in the painting sprang to life. They came across fierce soldiers, learned thinkers, and ethereal historical beings.

They were directed to the next hint by the characters, who said that the real treasure was the knowledge and insight obtained from the experiences of those who had come before.

The third clue guided them to a secret cave that was home to sparkling crystals and dazzling water pools. They came upon mirrors of themselves, each displaying events from their life, as they went deeper into the cave.

They learned important lessons from their reflections on their qualities, flaws, and the beauty of their uniqueness. The youngsters came to understand that the actual value resided not in the material wealth they coveted, but rather in the individual characteristics that made each of them different.

The last hint brought them back to the old cemetery, where they were confronted with a large, venerable tree. Its roots extended far into the ground, while its branches reached towards the sky.

In a calming voice, the tree said, "Congratulations, young explorers. You found the actual purpose of the treasure by following the directions on the ghostly treasure hunt map.

Emily said with her eyes wide with intrigue, "But what is the treasure?"

"The treasure is the memories you create together, the wisdom you gain from the past, the knowledge of who you are, and the bond of friendship that unites you all," the tree retorted.

The tree said, "And just like this old tree, your friendship will grow stronger with each passing year."Keep in mind to value one another, be there for one another, and enjoy the magic of Halloween every day."

The kids were happy as they expressed gratitude to the old tree for its knowledge. Despite not producing monetary wealth, the spectral treasure hunt had filled their hearts and souls with the real jewels of life.

They knew they had been through something special as they headed back to Spookville. They had discovered that Halloween's genuine charm rested not in pursuing outward pleasures but rather in embracing the spirit of exploration and the strength of camaraderie.

So, my readers, keep in mind the story of the Ghostly Treasure Hunt while you celebrate Halloween this year. Accept life's mysteries, look for lessons from the past, and enjoy the friendships that brighten every day.

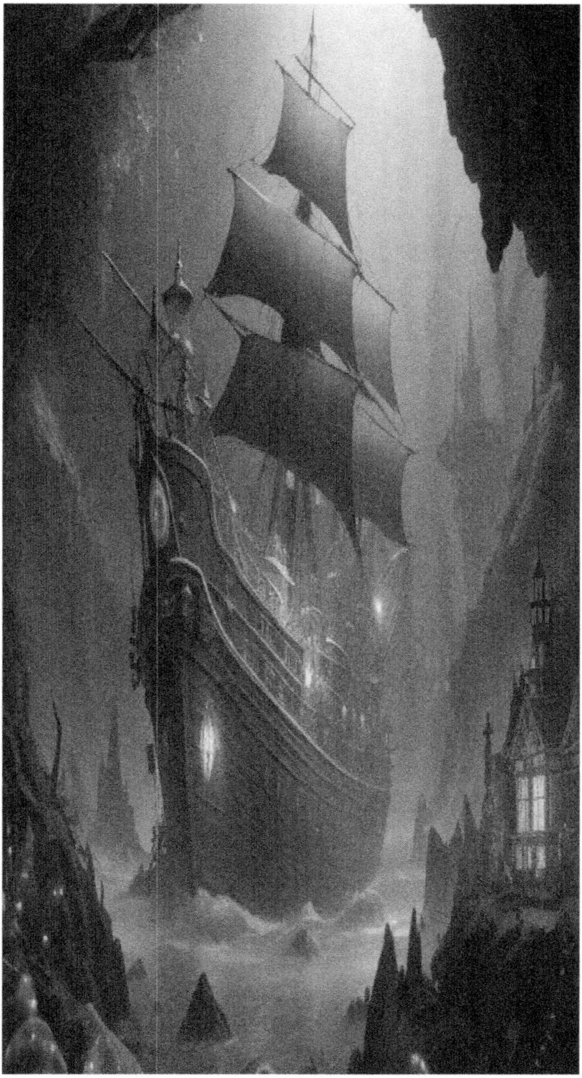

THE SPECTRAL MASQUERADE BALL

A Strange invitation flew into the hands of Alex, Lily, Emily, Charlie, and Mike as Halloween night continued its wonderful dance. You are warmly welcomed to the Spectral Masquerade Ball, read the invitation, which was exquisitely made and embellished with silver filigree.

The youngsters were intrigued and thrilled as they followed the cryptic instructions on the invitation, which took them to a large, old estate outside of Spookville. The home appeared before them as an eerie grandeur, its windows lit up by a captivating light.

The moment they entered, they were confronted with an amazing scene. The estate had been turned into a fantasy setting, complete with crystal chandeliers in the ballrooms and purple, silver, and gold accents everywhere.

The ballroom was filled with masked people skillfully twirling and dancing, their laughter ringing out like tinkling bells. Each person appeared to be hiding an identity behind a distinctive mask.

They came to understand that the attendees were not just regular partygoers but were ethereal entities such as ghosts, fairies, witches, and creatures of the night as they interacted with them. The Spectral Masquerade Ball brought together supernatural beings from other worlds.

A towering person dressed in a blanket of stars greeted them like a courteous host. He greeted them with a royal attitude, "Welcome to the Spectral Masquerade Ball." You may be anyone you want to be tonight. Accept transformation's magic and allow your genuine selves show.

The kids put on their magical masks with his words in mind, and as they did, they noticed a subtle change in themselves. They were no longer merely kids from Spookville, but rather fantastical beings eager to take part in the enchantment of the night.

They joined the dance as the night went on, swaying to the tunes that appeared to be from another world. Under the starry sky, they danced with elegant fairies, waltzed with phantom dancers, and swirled with fantastical animals.

The enigmatic Lady Aurora, a ghostly apparition with eyes that could see the secrets of the stars, appeared to them in the midst of the festivities. The Spectral Masquerade Ball is a celebration of Halloween's spirit as well as a night of magic, she said in a voice like a soft wind.

The lines between realms are fuzzy tonight, said Lady Aurora. "It is a night where the supernatural essence embraces the spirit of humanity and where the magical and the everyday dance together."

The kids listened in astonishment as they understood that Halloween was a celebration of the wonders that existed outside the realm of reality and not just a night of eerie thrills.

As night fell, Lady Aurora made a spectacular announcement about a fireworks show that would fill the night sky with magical and colorful bursts. As magical animals and scenarios from their wildest thoughts appeared in the pyrotechnics, the kids watched in awe.

The courteous host congratulated the kids for attending the event as the Spectral Masquerade Ball came to an end. Remember that this night's charm is not limited to this mansion, he said with a smile. Bring the Halloween spirit with you and may it guide you through the darkest of times.

They understood that the Spectral Masquerade Ball had been more than just a night of fun as they said goodbye to the magical home and its ghostly occupants. A window into the worlds of wonder and imagination that each of them contained, it had been a transforming experience.

They were in awe and thankful as they made their way back to Spookville. They had learned from Halloween that enchantment may be found in both the fantastical and mundane aspects of life.

So, my readers, keep in mind the story of the Spectral Masquerade Ball while you celebrate Halloween this year. Accept the magic of change, rejoice in the Halloween spirit, and may the magic of this night light your life tonight and always.

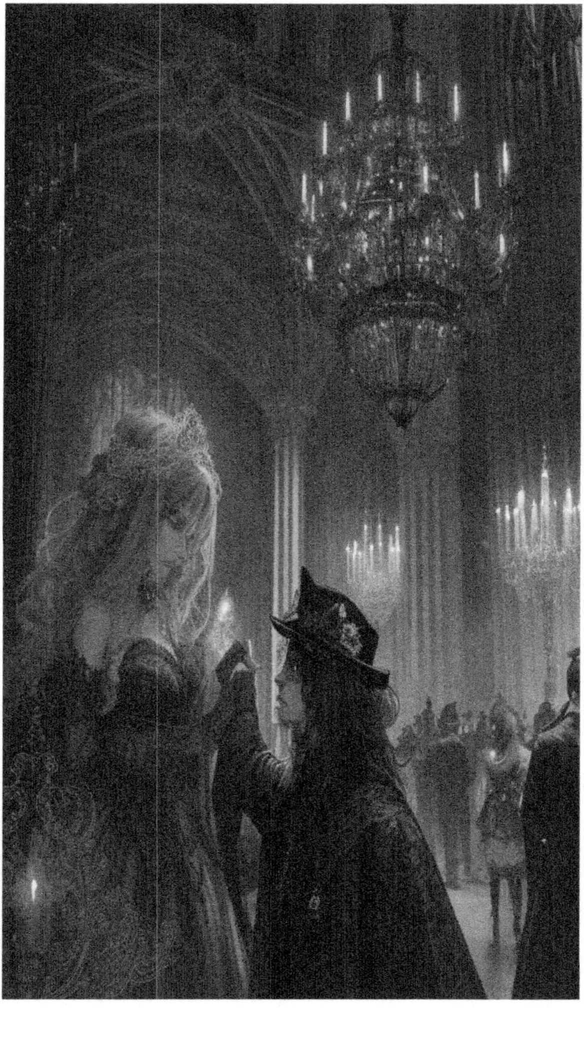

SECRET OF THE CREEPY MANSION

A Terrifying tale about a Creepy Mansion that had magically emerged on the outskirts of town began to circulate among the kids as the moon hung low in the night sky and threw an ominous glow over Spookville. The mansion was large and intimidating, with its gates bolted shut and its windows boarded up. Alex, Lily, Emily, Charlie, and Mike were intrigued by the rumors of ghostly figures and eerie whispers circulating around the estate.

The kids took their torches and embarked on a moonlit excursion, determined to learn the mysteries of the Creepy Mansion. They continued despite the thorny vines and tangled branches along the route to the mansion, propelled by a mix of exhilaration and terror.

The air seemed to get colder as they got closer to the home, and there was an unsettling silence all around. The mansion towered above them like a ghost from another era, its deteriorating walls and discolored paint contributing to its eerie aura.

They cautiously opened the rusted gate and proceeded onto the overgrown grounds of the estate. Their spines tingled at the sound of the rustling leaves and the creaking floors. However, they persisted because their curiosity overcame their dread.

They were met by an unearthly scene as they approached the home. Cobwebs covered the great entrance, and the dusty chandelier swung as if moved by an invisible power. The children's footfall gave the house an unsettling pulse as they reverberated through the empty halls.

They discovered a secret door during their search that led to a forgotten chamber. Dusty furniture and outdated photographs were everywhere in the space. They discovered a painting of a historical family among the portraits. The family noticed that the painting's characters seemed to be watching them from every angle and that they had an unexplainable bond with them.

They found a journal hidden in a dingy drawer as they searched more. The journal belonged to Isabella, a young woman who had lived at the home decades earlier. The journal entries related a harrowing story of sad secrets, lost loves, and a curse that had befallen the home.

They discovered that Isabella had a crush on Nathaniel, a young guy, but that their relationship had been disallowed because of a family dispute. Isabella had turned to a strange person in desperation after losing her family, who had promised to lift the curse.

The diary mentioned a lost treasure that may remove the curse and release the wandering spirits imprisoned within the walls of the home. The kids were aware that they had to locate the treasure in order to solve the riddles surrounding the Creepy Mansion.

They set off on a dangerous expedition within the home, following the hints in the journal as they encountered haunting apparitions and terrifying illusions that put their courage to the test. They came upon Isabella and Nathaniel's restless souls, who begged them to aid in removing the spell binding them.

They eventually found the buried treasure, a mysterious pendant that shone with a flimsy, ethereal light, as they dug further into the mansion's mysteries. Lifting the curse and freeing the spirits depended on the amulet.

They went back to the image of Isabella's family with the amulet in hand and set it on it. The mansion shook and the spirits of Isabella and Nathaniel were freed from their unending torture as the amulet started to glow brightly.

The youngsters marveled as the crumbling walls of the home were brought back to their former splendor. The house appeared to come alive with a sudden life when the boarded-up windows disappeared.

They were met by Isabella and Nathaniel, whose expressions were ones of appreciation. Isabella remarked with a voice choked with emotion, "Thank you for helping us break the curse and find peace.

Knowing that Isabella and Nathaniel had discovered the Creepy Mansion's mystery and put an end to the ghosts' agitation, the kids bade them farewell. They left the home with a sense of success and a renewed understanding for the secrets that lie concealed across the universe.

As they made their way back to Spookville, they realized that Halloween was more than just a night of spooks and chills; it was also a night for uncovering mysteries, embracing the uncharted, and finding the enchantment hidden in every nook and cranny of life.

So, my readers, keep in mind the story of The Secret of the Creepy Mansion while you celebrate Halloween this year. Let the enchantment of the night lead you on your own amazing experiences as you embrace the wonders all around you, face your anxieties head-on, and do so.

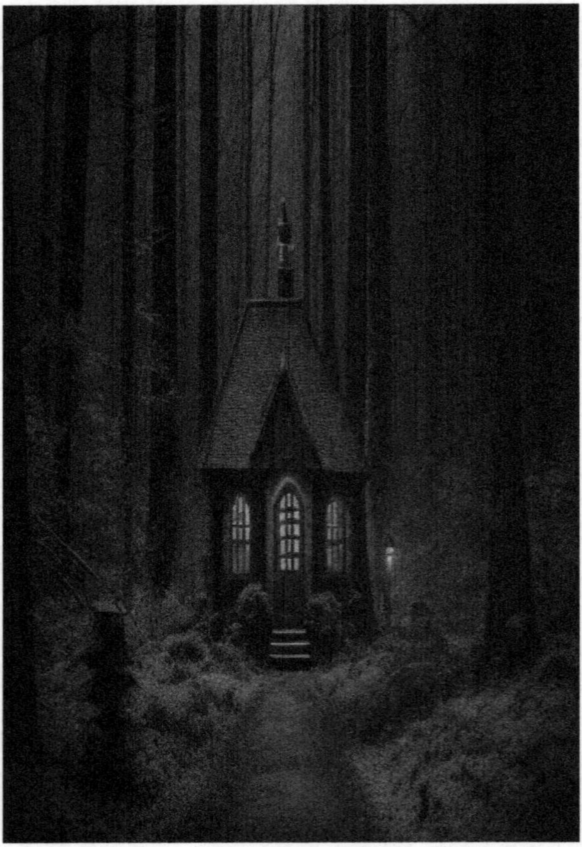

THE NIGHT OF THE LIVING TOYS

A Strange event started to take place as Halloween night proceeded to fascinate Spookville. The town's toy store's previously lifeless toys appeared to come to life, their eyes shining with a spooky light. The kids in Spookville marveled as the toys danced and played together as though they were having their own little Halloween celebration.

A gentle, melodious music drifted through the air among the spellbinding scene. The youngsters were lured by the eerie tune to the center of the toy store, where an old music box was perched on a dingy shelf.

The toys moved with even more grace and elegance as Alex delicately wound the music box when their curiosity got the better of them. The melody evoked memories of magical childhood moments and long-forgotten dreams.

The toys suddenly stopped moving, and a gentle, ethereal glow came from the music box. When it opened, a little, worn parchment was hidden within. The parchment was written with a beautiful riddle that appeared to invite the reader to go forth on a wondrous journey.

"Look for the treasure where shadows take flight to solve the enigma of this night. Follow the moon's silver radiance to the place where living toys' secrets are bestowed.

The youngsters were intrigued by the mystery and knew they had to follow the moon's light to learn the truth about the Night of the Living Toys.

They continued along the moonlit road, which took them right to the center of the magical woodland. With moonbeams weaving like silver threads through the trees, the forest—normally a haven of wonder and joy—seemed to carry an eerie air.

As they continued on, they came to a clearing that was bathed in the silvery glory of the moon. A grand tree with luminous toys that appeared to dance like fireflies stood in the middle of the scene. Each toy had a little lamp that cast a magical glow over the clearing.

It's like a fantastic toy wonderland, Emily murmured.

As the kids got closer to the tree, a ghostly apparition emerged from the darkness. It was the Guardian of the Toys, a legendary figure that guarded young people's fantasies and the wonder of childhood.

The figure spoke in a voice that rang with wisdom, "I am the Guardian of the Toys." "Tonight, the toys have come alive to celebrate the Halloween spirit and the wonder of imagination."

The Guardian wrote, "You solved the puzzle and released the music box's enchantment. The Night of the Living Toys is about to give you the gift of never-ending wonder.

Small, intricate keys with an ethereal sheen were handed to them by the Guardian. These keys have the ability to release the toys' charm and preserve the essence of childhood in your hearts.

The kids took the keys with thankfulness and astonishment in their hearts. They were aware that the Night of the Living Toys had bestowed upon them a gift beyond all hope: the ability to never outgrow childish marvels.

With the keys in their possession, they went back to the toy store where the toys had already returned to their original locations and were now once more appearing as inanimate playthings.

The toys came to life for one last time as the clock struck midnight, waving and bowing to the kids as they left.

The toys all chimed together, "Thank you for sharing in the enchantment of this night with us.

The kids grinned, their hearts brimming with surprise and happiness. They were aware that the Night of the Living Toys had been a night of enduring wonder and enchantment, serving as a reminder that childhood magic persisted as they aged.

So, my readers, keep in mind the story of the Night of the Living Toys while you celebrate Halloween this year. Celebrate the wonders of childhood, embrace the magic of creativity, and May the magic of Halloween continue to dance in your hearts forever.

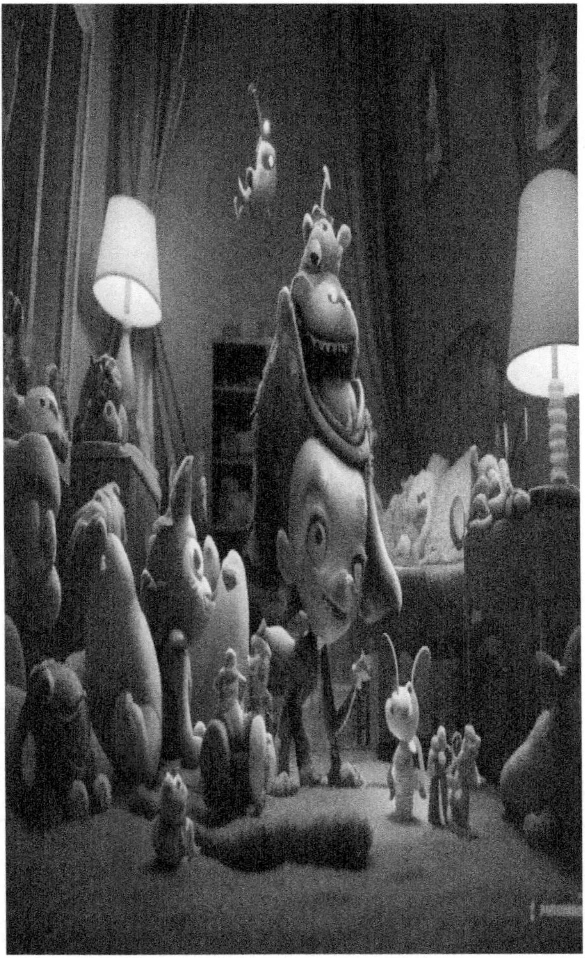

THE HAUNTED HAYRIDE ADVENTURE

A Strange sight came at the outside of town as Halloween night continued to enchant Spookville: a ghostly hayride drawn by haunting horses, its carriage decked up with blazing pumpkins and unsettling lanterns. The youngsters of Spookville joyfully boarded the scary hayride after succumbing to its charm.

They traveled through the eerie, ominous woodlands on the hayride, where the shadows appeared to dance in the moonlight. They could hear the distant howling of unknown beasts and the rustle of leaves as they walked farther into the woods.

They observed phantom creatures moving through the woods amid the cold atmosphere. In the darkness, these were the ghosts of Spookville's past, joining the hayride to celebrate Halloween.

They were particularly drawn to the Ghost of Captain William Turner, a renowned pirate who formerly prowled the waters close to Spookville. His ghostly body was dressed in ragged pirate garb, and his eyes sparkled with a sense of adventure.

"Ahoy, you young explorers!" Captain Turner shouted while grinning slyly. You've gotten on the Haunted Hayride Adventure, where on this eerie night, the stories of the high seas come to life.

They set off on a fascinating tour through Spookville's eerie history with Captain Turner as their guide. They navigated the moonlight lake, where the ghosts of drowned sailors rose from the water's depths and swayed to the sound of the waves.

They then entered the historic cemetery, where old gravestones murmured stories of lost love and unfulfilled hopes.

The departed souls danced amid the graves as their recollections were woven into the night's atmosphere.

They arrived at a haunting village where ghostly beings were joyously celebrating a long-forgotten festival as the hayride proceeded. The youngsters had the impression that they had entered a bygone period as the hamlet was alive with eerie music and laughing.

They were fascinated by the spooky stories that played out in front of them as they watched each scene, learning more about the past and mythology of Spookville.

The hayride took them to an ancient, deserted lighthouse placed on a cliff overlooking the sea, marking the culmination of their quest. They saw a phantom fight between pirates and mythical sea monsters as the lighthouse's beam of light swept over the horizon.

"This be the final challenge, young explorers," Captain Turner roared.

Assume control of the situation by taking on the sea spirits.

The youngsters joined the spectral pirates in their conflict with the sea animals with a newfound boldness. They bravely and resolutely battled off the ethereal adversaries while brandishing fictitious weapons.

The marine animals disappeared into the waves as the conflict grew fierce, and the pirates hailed their victory. You've shown yourselves worthy of this ghostly expedition, Captain Turner smirked at the kids.

On the spooky journey back to Spookville, the kids experienced awe and a sense of achievement. Along with being an exciting adventure, the Haunted Hayride Adventure took them through the past and folklore of their home town.

Captain Turner and the other spectral characters were bid farewell by the group, who knew they had been given a once-in-a-lifetime opportunity to witness a night of living stories and a window into the mysteries that surrounded them.

So, my readers, keep in mind the story of the Haunted Hayride Adventure while you enjoy Halloween this year. Take in the beauties of your environment, embrace the enchantment of narrative, and May the spirit of exploration always lead you on your own ghostly travels.

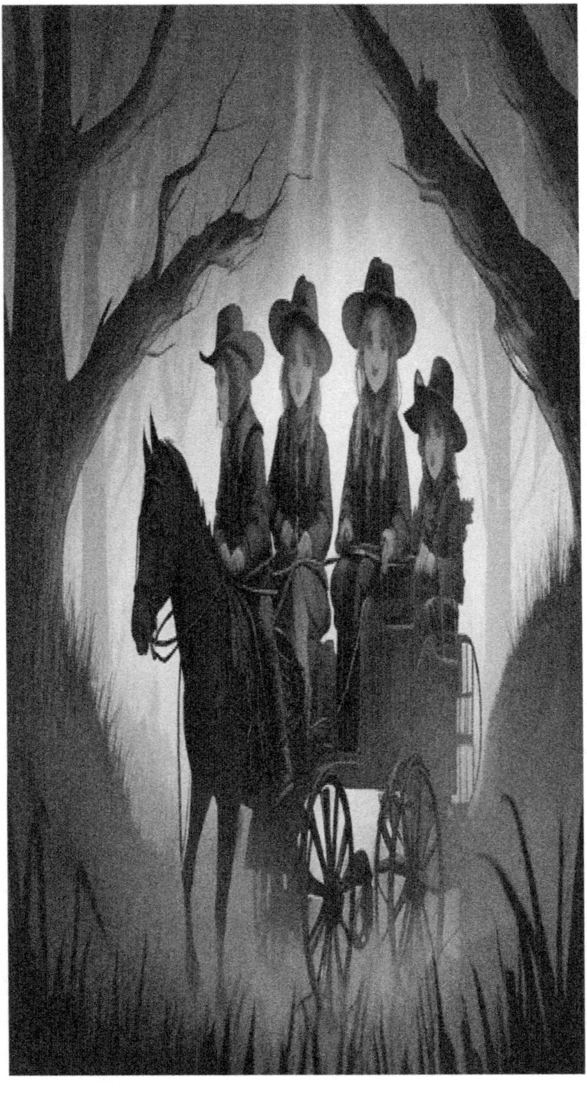

THE GHOST SHIP IN MOONLIGHT BAY

Children in Spookville began to talk about a famous Ghost Ship that only showed up on the darkest of nights as Halloween night came to a crescendo. The spectral crew of the Ghost Ship was thought to be permanently stuck in the world of the living, and it was reported to sail the seas of Moonlight Bay with its torn sails blowing in the wind.

Alex, Lily, Emily, Charlie, and Mike were intrigued by the Ghost Ship legend and made the decision to travel to Moonlight Bay to experience the eerie spectacle for themselves.

A location of magic and mystery, Moonlight Bay was renowned for its waters' silver hue, which shimmered in the moonlight. The fog was rolling in as the kids arrived to the bay, providing an ethereal atmosphere that contributed to the feeling of otherworldly suspense.

The Ghost Ship then materialized there, looming like a ghost from the past, just as the tales had predicted. As it navigated the foggy seas, its torn sails flapped in the wind and its hull squeaked.

The phantom crew of the ship emerged from the shadows as they stared in wonder. Each member of the team was dressed in vintage clothing, and a perpetual look of desire could be seen on their features.

One person in particular caught their attention: Captain Greybeard, the fabled leader of the Ghost Ship. His once-majestic beard had gone ghostly white, and his eyes sparkled with a deep sadness.

With a voice that echoed through the ages, Captain Greybeard welcomed the youthful adventurers to the Ghost Ship at Moonlight Bay. We are lost souls destined to navigate these seas eternally because we are trapped between the living and the dead.

The kids listened sympathetically as they realized that the crew of the Ghost Ship were not evil ghosts but rather lost souls seeking peace from their unending misery.

Captain Greybeard said, "We were once valiant sailors, pursuing the riches of far-off countries. The genuine joys of life, such as love, friendship, and the joy of the present moment, however, were overlooked in our chase of material wealth.

The youngsters felt sympathy spring up in their hearts as they realized the captain's anguish. They understood that finding the immaterial treasures that really counted, as opposed to worldly wealth, held the key to ending the Ghost Ship's curse.

They recounted tales of friendship and love, of mishaps and adventures, as well as the pleasures and difficulties they encountered in Spookville, with a fresh zeal.

The Ghost Ship appeared to be emitting a soft, shimmering glow while they talked. The crew's moods started to lift, and there was a feeling of optimism in the air.

With a mix of melancholy and optimism, Captain Greybeard replied, "We have been tortured by regrets and unrealized hopes. But your descriptions of Spookville's exploits have served to remind us of the beauty of life and the value of savoring the moment.

Captain Greybeard said a sincere thank you to the kids and waved them off. The ghostly crew of the Ghost Ship found comfort in the knowledge that their stories would always live on in the hearts of the living as it gradually faded into the mist.

The kids realized they had gone through something spectacular as they stood on Moonlight Bay's shores. The Ghost Ship at Moonlight Bay served as both an eerie spectacle and a sobering reminder of how short life is and how important it is to live in the now.

They had a newfound respect for Halloween's charm and the delights of Spookville when they returned. They were aware that the ghost of the Ghost Ship will always be with them, serving as a reminder to cherish their time together.

So, my readers, keep in mind the story of the Ghost Ship at Moonlight Bay as you celebrate Halloween this year. Cherish the memories of the past, embrace the beauty of the present, and may Halloween's enchantment always serve as a beacon for your own remarkable travels.

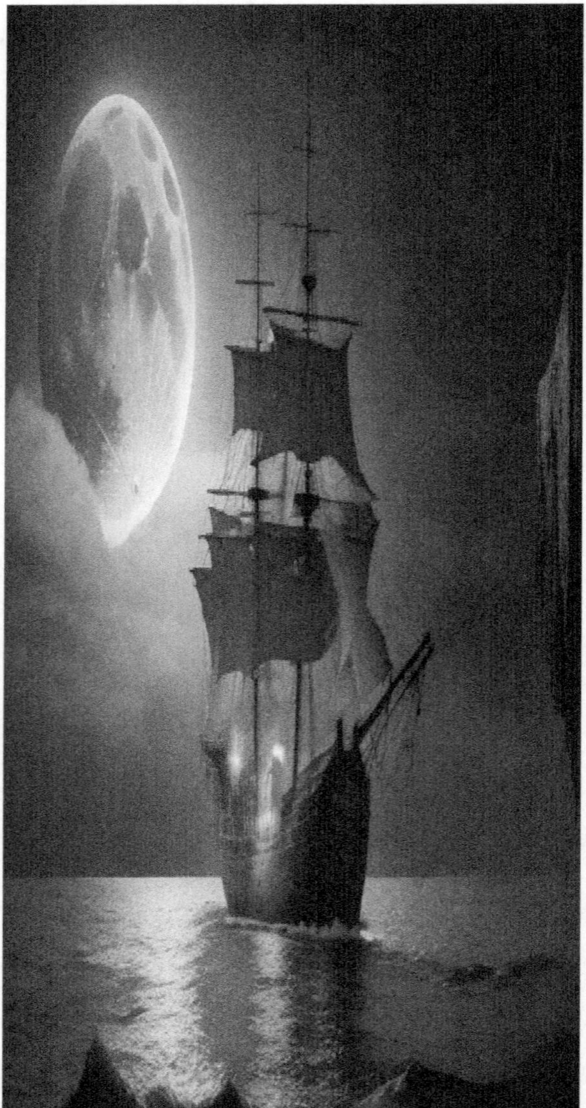

Printed in Great Britain
by Amazon